how can one sell the air?

Chief Seattle's Vision

THE BOOK PUBLISHING COMPANY
SUMMERTOWN, TENNESSEE

ISBN 0-913990-48-5

THE BOOK PUBLISHING COMPANY • PO Box 99 • Summertown, TN 38483

Copyright © 1992
Author: Chief Seattle
Editors: Eli Gifford and R. Michael Cook
Illustrations and design by Eleanor Dale Evans

William Arrowsmith's adaptation of Chief Seattle's speech is included with permission from his estate.
Ted Perry's script for the movie HOME is included with Mr. Perry's permission.
Cover photograph of Chief Seattle used with permission of *Suquamish Tribal Photographic Archives*.

How can one sell the air? : Chief Seattle's Vision / [editors, Eli Gifford and R.
    Michael Cook].
                p.   cm.
        Includes bibliographical references.
        Contents: Chief Seattle's speech as recorded by Dr. Henry Smith (1854,
published 1887) -- Historical information and background -- [Speech] by
Ted Perry, inspired by Chief Seattle -- Adaptation by William Arrowsmith.
        ISBN 0-913990-48-5 : $6.95
        1. Seattle, Chief, 1790-1866--Oratory. 2. Speeches, addresses, etc.,
Suquamish. 3. Suquamish Indians--Land tenure. 4. Human ecology. I.
Seattle, Chief, 1790-1866. II. Gifford, Eli, 1951-. III. Cook, R. Michael,
1950-.
E99.S85H68 1992
979.7'004979--dc20
                                                92-44235
                                                CIP

10 9 8 7

2

This book is printed with soy-based ink on recycled paper.

The illustrations in this book are representative of all native peoples in North America.

Ted Perry and the estate of William Arrowsmith have generously donated their portions of the proceeds of this book to the Suquamish Nation. In addition, *The Book Publishing Company* will donate part of the profits from this book to the Suquamish.

HOW CAN ONE SELL THE AIR?

Yonder sky that has wept tears of passion

Spoken by Chief Seattle
and recorded by Dr. Henry Smith in 1854
Published in the Seattle Sunday Star, October 29, 1887

Yonder sky that has wept tears of compassion on our fathers for centuries untold,
and which to us, looks eternal, may change.
Today it is fair,
tommorrow it may be overcast with clouds.
My words are like stars that never set.
What Seattle says, the great chief, Washington can rely upon,
with as much certainty as our pale-face brothers can rely upon the return of the seasons.

The son of the white chief says his father sends us greetings of friendship and good will.
This is kind, for we know he has little need of our friendship in return,
because his people are many.
They are like the grass that covers the vast prairies,
while my people are few,
and resemble the scattering trees of a storm-swept plain.

The great, and I presume also good, white chief sends us word that he wants to buy our land but is willing to allow us to reserve enough to live on comfortably.
This indeed appears generous, for the red man no longer has rights that he need respect, and the offer may be wise, also, for we are no longer in need of a great country.

9

THERE WAS A TIME
when our people covered the whole land,
 as the waves of a wind-ruffled sea
cover its shell-paved floor.
But that time has long since passed away
with the greatness of tribes now almost forgotten.
I will not mourn over our untimely decay,
nor reproach my pale-face brothers for hastening it,
for we, too, may have been somewhat to blame.

When our young men grow angry
at some real or imaginary wrong,
and disfigure their faces with black paint,
their hearts, also, are disfigured and turn black,
and then their cruelty is relentless
and knows no bounds,
and our old men are not able to restrain them.

But let us hope that hostilities
between the red-man and his pale-face brothers
may never return.
We would have everything to lose
and nothing to gain.

True it is, that revenge,
with our young braves,
is considered gain,
even at the cost of their own lives,
but old men who stay at home in times of war,
and old women, who have sons to lose,
know better.

Our great father Washington, for I presume he is now our father as well as yours,
since George has moved his boundaries to the north;
our great and good father, I say, sends us word by his son,
who, no doubt, is a great chief among his people,
that if we do as he desires, he will protect us.
His brave armies will be to us a bristling wall of strength,
and his great ships of war will fill our harbors
so that our ancient enemies far to the northward,
the Simsiams and Hydas
will no longer frighten our women and old men.
Then he will be our father and we will be his children.

BUT CAN THIS EVER BE?
Your God loves your people and hates mine;
he folds his strong arms lovingly around the white man
and leads him as a father leads his infant son,
but he has forsaken his red children;
he makes your people wax strong every day,
and soon they will fill the land;
while my people are ebbing away like a fast-receding tide,
that will never flow again.
The white man's God cannot love his red children
or he would protect them.
They seem to be orphans
and can look nowhere for help.
How can we become brothers?
How can your father become our father
and bring us prosperity
and awaken in us dreams of returning greatness?

Your God seems to us to be partial.
He came to the white man.
We never saw Him.
We never even heard His voice:
He gave the white man laws
but He had no word for His red children
whose teeming millions filled this vast continent
as the stars fill the firmament.
No, we are two distinct races
and must ever remain so.
There is little in common between us.
The ashes of our ancestors are sacred
and their final resting place is hallowed ground,
while you wander away from the tombs
of your fathers seemingly without regret.

Your religion was written on tables of stone by the iron finger of an angry God, lest you might forget it. The red-man could never remember nor comprehend it.

Our religion is the traditions of our ancestors, the dreams of our old men, given them by the great Spirit, and the visions of our sachems, and is written in the hearts of our people.

Your dead cease to love you and the homes of their nativity
as soon as they pass the portals of the tomb.
They wander far off beyond the stars,
are soon forgotten,
and never return.
Our dead never forget the beautiful world that gave them being.
They still love its winding rivers, its great mountains and its sequestered vales,
and they ever yearn in tenderest affection over the lonely hearted living
and often return to visit and comfort them.

Day and night cannot dwell together.
The red man has ever fled the approach of the white man,
as the changing mists on the mountain side flee before the blazing morning sun.

However, your proposition seems a just one, and I think my folks will accept it
and will retire to the reservation you offer them,
and we will dwell apart and in peace,
for the words of the great white chief seem to be the voice of nature
speaking to my people out of the thick darkness that is fast gathering around them
like a dense fog floating inward from a midnight sea.

It matters but little where we pass the remainder of our days.

THEY ARE NOT MANY.

The Indian's night promises to be dark.
No bright star hovers about the horizon.
Sad-voiced winds moan in the distance.
Some grim Nemsis of our race is on the red man's trail,
and wherever he goes he will still hear the sure approaching footsteps of the fell destroyer
and prepare to meet his doom,
as does the wounded doe that hears the approaching footsteps of the hunter.
A few more moons, a few more winters
and not one of all the mighty hosts that once filled this broad land
or that now roam in fragmentary bands through these vast solitudes
will remain to weep over the tombs of a people once as powerful and as hopeful as your own.

But why should we repine?
Why should I murmur at the fate of my people?
Tribes are made up of individuals and are no better than they.
Men come and go like the waves of the sea.
A tear, a tamanawus, a dirge, and they are gone from our longing eyes forever.
Even the white man,
whose God walked and talked with him, as friend to friend,
is not exempt from the common destiny.
We may be brothers after all.
We shall see.

We will ponder your proposition,
and when we have decided we will tell you.
But should we accept it,
I here and now make this first condition:
That we will not be denied the privilege,
without molestation,
of visiting at will
the graves of our ancestors and friends.
Every part of this country is sacred to my people.
Every hill-side, every valley,
every plain and grove
has been hallowed
by some fond memory
or sad experience of my tribe.

20

EVEN THE ROCKS
that seem to lie dumb
as they swelter in the sun along the silent seashore
in solemn grandeur
thrill with memories of past events
connected with the fate of my people,
and the very dust under your feet
responds more lovingly to our footsteps than to yours,
because it is the ashes of our ancestors,
and our bare feet are conscious of the sympathetic touch,
for the soil is rich with the life of our kindred.

The sable braves, and fond mothers, and glad-hearted maidens,
and the little children who lived and rejoiced here,
and whose very names are now forgotten,
still love these solitudes,
and their deep fastnesses at eventide
grow shadowy with the presence of dusky spirits.
And when the last red man
shall have perished from the earth
and his memory among white man
shall have become a myth,
these shores shall swarm with the invisible dead of my tribe,
and when your children's children
shall think themselves alone
in the field, the store, the shop, upon the highway
or in the silence of the woods,
they will not be alone.
In all the earth there is no place dedicated to solitude.
At night, when the streets of your cities and villages
shall be silent, and you think them deserted,
they will throng with the returning hosts
that once filled and still love this beautiful land.
The white man will never be alone.

22

Let him be just and deal kindly with my people,
for the dead are not altogether powerless.

Historical Information and Background

In recent years there has been much debate about Chief Seattle's speech. The main controversy centers around the authenticity of the version of the speech most popularly attributed to him. Although we may never know exactly what Chief Seattle said, we believe that he was probably as eloquent as subsequent versions of his speech portray him to be.

Seattle (more correctly "Seathl" or "Sealth") was the son of a Suquamish chief, Schweabe, whose people lived around Puget Sound in Washington State. His mother, Scholitza, was the daughter of a Duwamish chief. Because the line of descendants follows matrilineally, Seathl was considered Duwamish. As a young warrior he was renowned for his courage, daring, and leadership. While Seathl was a young chief, he gained control of six of the local tribes. Through the years, he continued the friendly relations his father had established with the local whites. By the time Chief Seathl gave his speech, he was in his late fifties or early sixties.

Eli Gifford, a history teacher with an M.A. in U.S. History, has done an in-depth study on the origins of this speech. Along with a number of other researchers, Mr. Gifford has traced the origin and evolution of the speech and writings it has inspired.

According to Gifford, Chief Seathl gave his now-famous speech to Isaac I. Stevens, the new Governor and Commissioner of Indian Affairs for the Washington Territories on January 10, 1854, while Stevens was on a preliminary field trip "to visit and take a census of the Indian tribes, and learn something of the character of the sound and its harbor." (Hazard Stevens, *The Life of Isaac Ingalls Stevens* Vol. 1, NY: Houghton, Mifflin Co. 1901 pp. 416-417)

One of the people in attendance at the meeting was Dr. Henry Smith, who took extensive notes on Seathl's speech, although those notes have never been found. Dr. Smith had lived in the area for two years and had a keen interest in the local Indians. He hired Indian laborers to help on his farm and had a working knowledge of Chinnok jargon (a trade language of about 300 words that was used by the Native Americans and whites). Seathl delivered his speech in his native tongue, Lushotseed. From Lushotseed it was translated to Chinnok jargon; it was then translated into English. This process greatly simplified Seathl's message.

The first printed version of the speech was written by Dr. Smith and appeared in the October 29, 1887 edition of the *Seattle Sunday Star* in an article entitled "Early Reminiscences Number Ten, Scraps from a Diary." This speech (see pages 7-23) presents Seathl's message in a flowery Victorian style, more typical of Smith's background than Seathl's. However, after consultation with the elders of their tribe in 1982, members of the Suquamish Museum determined Smith's version to be the most accurate account of Seathl's speech.

In the late 1960s, William Arrowsmith, a professor of classical literature at the University of Texas, came across a paragraph of Smith's version of Seathl's speech. He was struck by the similarities between Seathl's words and works by the Greek poet, Pindar. Inspired by his findings, Arrowsmith decided to take Dr. Smith's version of the speech and reedit it, using the language and phrasing more commonly spoken by regional tribes in Seathl's time. By talking to the traditional elders of these tribes, Arrowsmith was able to develop a sense of the syntax they used. We have included the professor's version on pages 57-77.

The most well-known version of Seathl's speech was written by Ted Perry, a theater arts professor and playwright at the University of Texas and a good friend of Arrowsmith's. This version of the speech can be found on pages 31-55. Perry was under contract to the Southern Baptist's Radio and Television Commission to write several films on topics of his choosing, including one on the contamination of our planet. In 1970 Perry attended an Earth Day rally at the University of Texas where he heard Arrowsmith read his version of the speech. With Arrowsmith's permission, Perry used the text as the basis for a new, fictitious speech which served as the narration for a film on pollution and ecology called *Home*. John Stevens was the film's producer. In an interview with Eli Gifford, Stevens said his job was to edit films and adapt them to meet the interests of the Southern Baptist Radio and Television Commission. Without notifying Perry, Stevens revised the text, added phrases referring to God, and the line "I am a savage and do not understand." Also, without Perry's knowledge or permission, the film's credits stated that the script was a speech spoken by Chief Seathl and gave no credit or acknowledgment to the fact that Perry had, in fact, written it. Perry had told Stevens the narration was *adapted* from a speech by Seathl. Stevens credited Perry by saying the script was researched by Ted Perry. In a phone interview with Eli Gifford on April 1, 1995, Stevens said that by leaving his name and Perry's name off the credits, "it would give the script more authenticity. . . . I thought by using the word *adapted*, it was fairly obvious it was not a word-for-word transcription." As a promotion for the movie *Home*, the Commission sent out 18,000 posters with their version of Perry's script, claiming it was a speech given by Chief Seathl. This was done without Stevens' knowledge or permission.

Environmental Action magazine published the Baptists' version of the speech in its November 11, 1972, issue. By this time, it was no longer a speech by Chief Seathl but had become a letter he sent to President Pierce. However, it was the publication of an article entitled "The Decidedly Unforked Message of Chief Seattle" in the Northwest Airlines magazine *Passages* that spread the Baptists' version nationally and internationally. The article's sidebar stated the "letter" was an "Adaptation of his [Seathl's] remarks based on an English translation by William Arrowsmith" and made no reference to Perry but did make reference to the Southern Baptist Radio and Television Commission.

~

We are aware that there are many other adaptations of Chief Seathl's speech. We hope the versions included in this book are, at least in part, representative of the spirit of Chief Seathl and his desire for all people to live in harmony with the earth. Our intentions in tracing the history of this speech is to be informative without diminishing the inspiration it has brought to many people.

how can one sell the air?

by Ted Perry
Inspired by Chief Seattle

Every part of this earth is sacred to my people.
Every shining pine needle,
every tender shore,
every vapor in the dark woods,
every clearing, and
every humming insect
arc holy
in the memory and experience of my people.

The sap which courses through the trees
carries the memories of the red man.

The white man's dead forget the country of their birth
when they walk among the stars.
Our dead never forget this beautiful earth,
for it is the mother of the red men.
Our dead always love and remember
the earth's swift rivers,
the silent footsteps of spring,
the sparkling ripples on the surface of the ponds,
the gaudy colors of the birds.
We are a part of the earth and it is a part of us.
The perfumed flowers are our sisters;
the deer, the horse, the great condor,
these are our brothers.
The rocky crests,
the juices in the meadows,
the body heat of the pony,
and man all belong to the same family.

So when the Great Chief in Washington sends word
that he wishes to buy our land,
he asks much of us.

What Chief Seattle says, the Great Chief in Washington can count on
as surely as our white brothers can count on the return of the seasons.
My words are like the stars.
They do not set.

Chief Washington also sends us words of friendship and goodwill.
This is kind of him.

So we will consider your offer to buy our land.
It will not be easy.
This land is sacred to us.
We take our pleasure in the woods and the dancing streams.
The water that moves in the brooks is not water but the blood of our ancestors.
If we sell you the land, you must remember that it is sacred to us,
and forever teach your children that it is sacred.
Each ghostly reflection in the clear water of the lakes
tells of events and memories in the life of my people.
The water's gurgle is the voice of my father's father.
The rivers are our brothers; they quench our thirst.
The rivers, between the tender arms of their banks,
carry our canoes where they will.

If we sell our land, you must remember,
and teach your children,
that the rivers are our brothers,
and yours,
and you must henceforth give the rivers the kindness you would give to any brother.

So Chief Seattle will consider the offer of Chief Washington.
We will consider.
The red man has always retreated before the advancing white man,
as the mist on the mountain slopes runs before the morning sun.
To us the ashes of our fathers are sacred.
Their graves are holy ground, and so these hills, these trees.
This portion of earth is consecrated to us.

38

The white man does not understand.
One portion of land is the same to him as the next,
for he is a wanderer who comes in the night
and borrows from the land whatever he needs.
The earth is not his brother, but his enemy,
and when he has won the struggle,
he moves on.
He leaves his father's graves behind, and he does not care.
He kidnaps the earth from his children.
And he does not care.
The father's graves and the children's birthright are forgotten by the white man,
who treats his mother the earth and his brother the sky
as things to be bought, plundered, and sold,
like sheep, bread, or bright beads.
In this way, the dogs of appetite will devour the rich earth
and leave only a desert.

The white man is like a snake who eats his own tail in order to live.
And the tail grows shorter and shorter.
Our ways are different from your ways. We do not live well in your cities,
which seem like so many black warts on the face of the earth.
The sight of the white man's cities pains the eyes of the red man
like the sunlight which stabs the eyes of one emerging from a dark cave.
There is no place in the white man's cities quiet enough to hear
the unfurling of leaves in Spring or the rustle of insects' wings.
In the white man's cities, one is always trying to outrun an avalanche.
The clatter only seems to pierce the ears.
But what is there to living if a man cannot hear the lonely cry of the thrush
or the arguments of the frogs around a pond at night?

But I am a red man and do not understand.
I prefer the wind darting over the face of a pond
and the smell of the wind itself,
cleansed by a midday rainshower.
The air is precious to the red man,
for all things share the same breath —
the beasts, the trees, and man,
they are all of the same breath.

41

The white man does not mind the foul air he breathes.
Like a man in pain for many days,
he is numb to the stench.

42

But if we sell our land,
you must remember that the air is precious to us,
and our trees, and the beasts.
The wind gives man his first breath
and receives his last sigh.
And if we sell you our land,
you will keep it apart and sacred,
as a place
where even the white man can go
to taste a wind sweetened by meadow flowers.

43

So we will consider your offer to buy our land.
If we decide to accept,
I will here and now make one condition:
the white man must treat the beasts
of this land as his brothers.

I have heard stories
of a thousand rotting buffaloes on the prairie,
left by the white men who shot them from a passing train.
I do not understand.
For us, the beasts are our brothers,
and we kill only to stay alive.
If we sell him this land,
the white man must do the same,
for the animals are our brothers.
What is man without the beast?
Even the earthworm keeps the earth soft
for man to walk upon.
If all the beasts were gone, men would die from great loneliness.
For whatever happens to the beasts, happens to man
for we are all of one breath.

44

We will consider your offer to buy our land.
Do not send men asking us to decide more quickly. We will decide in our time.
Should we accept, I here and now make this condition:
we will never be denied the right to walk softly over the graves of our fathers, mothers, and friends, nor
may the white man desecrate these graves.

The graves must always be open to the sunlight and the falling rain.
Then the water will fall gently upon the green sprouts
and seep slowly down to moisten the parched lips of our ancestors
and quench their thirst.

If we sell this land to you, I will make now this condition:
You must teach your children that the ground beneath their feet
responds more lovingly to our steps than to yours,
because it is rich with the lives of our kin.
Teach your children
what we have taught our children,
that the earth is our mother.
Whatever befalls the earth,
befalls the sons of the earth.
If men spit upon the ground,
they spit upon themselves.
This we know.
The earth does not belong to the white man,
the white man belongs to the earth.
This we know.
All things are connected
like the blood
which unites our family.
If we kill the snakes,
the field mice will multiply and destroy our corn.

All things are connected.
Whatever befalls the earth,
befalls the sons and daughters of the earth.
Man did not weave the web of life;
he is merely a strand in it.
Whatever he does to the web,
he does to himself.

No, day and night cannot live together.
We will consider your offer.
What is it
that the white man wishes to buy,
my people ask me?
The idea is strange to us.
How can you buy or sell the sky,
the warmth of the land,
the swiftness of the antelope?
How can we sell these things to you
and how can you buy them?
Is the earth yours to do with as you will,
merely because the red man
signs a piece of paper
and gives it to the white man?
If we do not own the freshness of the air
and the sparkle of the water,
how can you buy them from us?
Can you buy back the buffalo,
once the last one has died?

But we will consider your offer.
In his passing moment of strength,
the white man thinks that he is a god
who can treat his mother (the earth),
the rivers (which are his sisters),
and his red brothers, as he wishes.
But the man who would buy and sell his mother,
his brothers, and sisters
would also burn his children
to keep himself warm.

So we will consider your offer to buy our land.
Day and night cannot live together.
Your offer seems fair,
and I think my people will accept it
and go to the reservation you have for them.

We will live apart, and in peace.

Tribes are made of men, nothing more.
Men come and go,
like the waves of the sea.
The whites too shall pass;
perhaps sooner than all other tribes.
Continuing to contaminate his own bed,
the white man will one night suffocate in his own filth.

But in his perishing the white man will shine brightly,
fired by the strength of the god who brought him to this land
and for some special purpose gave him dominion over this land.
That destiny is a mystery to us,
for we do not understand what living becomes
when the buffalo are all slaughtered,
the wild horses all tamed,
the secret corners of the forest are heavy with the scent of many men,
and the view of the ripe hills blotted by talking wires.
Where is the thicket? Gone.
Where is the eagle? Gone.
And what is it to say goodbye to the swift pony and the hunt?
The end of living and the beginning of survival.

The white man's god gave him dominion over the beasts, the woods, and the red man,
for some special purpose, but that destiny is a mystery to the red man.
We might understand if we knew what it was that the white man dreams,
what hopes he describes to children on long winter nights,
what visions he burns onto their eyes so that they will wish for tomorrow.
The white man's dreams are hidden from us.
And because they are hidden, we will go our own way.

So we will consider your offer to buy our land.
If we agree, it will be to secure the reservation you have promised.
There, perhaps, we may live out our brief days as we wish.
There is little in common between us.

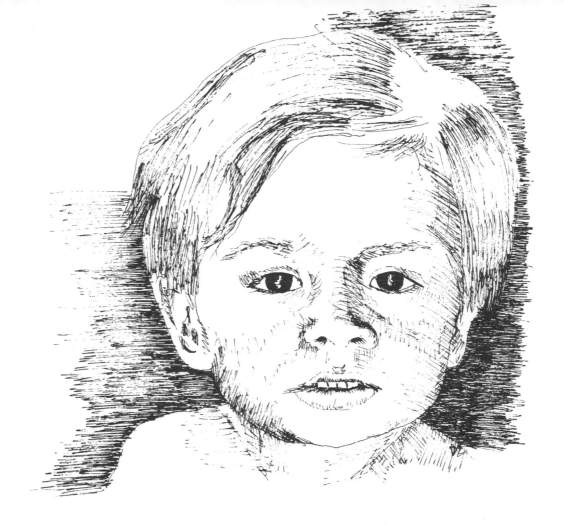

53

If we sell you our land,
it will be filled with the bold young men,
the warmbreasted mothers,
the sharp-minded women,
and the little children
who once lived and were happy here.

Your dead go to walk among the stars,
but our dead return to the earth they love.
The white man will never be alone unless,
in some distant day,
he destroys the mountains,
the trees, the rivers, and the air.
If the earth should come to that,
and the spirits of our dead,
who love the earth,
no longer wish to return
and visit their beloved,
then in that noon glare that pierces the eyes,
the white man will walk
his desert in great loneliness.

my words are like the stars

adapted by William Arrowsmith
from Chief Seattle's speech as recorded by Dr. Henry B. Smith

Brothers: That sky above us has pitied our fathers for many hundreds of years.
To us it looks unchanging, but it may change.
Today it is fair.
Tomorrow it may be covered with clouds.

My words are like the stars. They do not set.
What Seattle says, the great chief Washington can count on
as surely as our white brothers can count on the return of the seasons.

The White Chief's son says his father sends us words of friendship and good will.
This is kind of him, since we know he has little need of our friendship in return.
His people are many, like the grass that covers the plains.
My people are few, like the trees scattered by the storms on the grasslands.

The great — and good, I believe — White Chief sends us word that he wants to buy our land.
But he will reserve us enough so that we can live comfortably.
This seems generous, since the red man no longer has rights he needs to respect.
It may also be wise, since we no longer need a large country.
Once my people covered this land
like a flood-tide moving with the wind across the shell littered flats.
But that time is gone, and with it the greatness of tribes now almost forgotten.

But I will not mourn the passing of my people.
Nor do I blame our white brothers for causing it.
We too were perhaps partly to blame.
When our young men grow angry at some wrong,
real or imagined,
they make their faces ugly with black paint.
Then their hearts too are ugly and black.
They are hard and their cruelty knows no limits.
And our old men cannot restrain them.

Let us hope that the wars
between the red man and his white brothers
will never come again.
We would have everything to lose
and nothing to gain.
Young men view revenge as gain,
even when they lose their own lives.
But the old men
who stay behind in time of war,
mothers with sons to lose —
know better.

Our great father Washington —
for he must be our father now as well as yours, since George has moved his boundary northward —
our great and good father sends word by his son,
who is surely a great chief among his people,
that he will protect us if we do what he wants.
His brave soldiers will be a strong wall for my people,
and his great warships will fill our harbors.
Then our ancient enemies to the north — the Hadias and Tsimshians —
will no longer frighten our women and old men.
Then he will be our father and we will be his children.

But can that ever be?
Your God loves your people and hates mine.
He puts his strong arm around the white man
and leads him by the hand,
as a father leads his little boy.
He has abandoned his red children.
He makes your people stronger every day.
Soon they will flood all the land.
But my people are an ebb tide,
we never return.
No, the white man's God
cannot love his red children
or he would protect them.
Now we are orphans.
There is no one to help us.

So how can we be brothers?
How can your father be our father,
and make us prosper
and send us dreams of future greatness?
Your God is prejudiced.
He came to the white man.
We never saw him,
never even heard his voice.
He gave the white man laws,
but he had no word for his red children
whose numbers once filled this land
as the stars filled the sky.

No, we are two separate races,
and we must stay separate.
There is little in common between us.

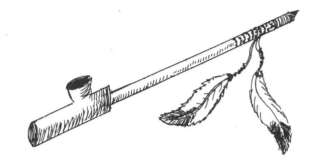

64

To us the ashes of our fathers are sacred.
Their graves are holy ground.
But you are wanderers,
you leave your fathers' graves behind you,
and you do not care.

65

Your religion was written on tables of stone
by the iron finger of an angry God,
so you would not forget it.
The red man could never understand it or remember it.
Our religion is the ways of our forefathers,
the dreams of our old men,
sent them by the Great Spirit, and visions of our sachems.
And it is written in the hearts of our people.

66

Your dead forget you and the country of their birth
as soon as they go beyond the grave and walk among the stars.
They are quickly forgotten and they never return.

Our dead never forget this beautiful earth.
It is their mother.
They always love and remember her rivers,
her great mountains, her valleys.
They long for the living,
who are lonely, too,
and who long for the dead.
And their spirits often return to visit and console us.

Day and night cannot dwell together.
The red man has ever fled the approach of the white man,
as the changing mists on the mountain side
flee before the blazing morning sun.

No, day and night cannot live together.

The red man has always retreated before the advancing white man,
as the mist on the mountain slopes runs before the morning sun.

So your offer seems fair, and I think my people will accept it
and go to the reservation you offer them.
We will live apart, and in peace.
For the words of the Great White Chief are like the words of nature
speaking to my people out of the great darkness
— a darkness that gathers around us like the night fog moving inland from a midnight sea.

It matters little where we pass the rest of our days.
They are not many.
The Indians' night will be dark.
No bright star shines on his horizons.
The wind is sad.
Fate hunts the red man down.
Wherever he goes, he will hear
the approaching steps of his destroyer,
and prepare to die,
like the wounded doe
who hears the step of the hunter.

A few more moons,
a few more winters,
and none of the children
of the great tribes that once lived in this wide earth
or that roam now in small bands in the woods
will be left to mourn the graves of a people
once as powerful and as hopeful as yours.

But why should I mourn the passing of my people?
Tribes are made of men,
nothing more.
Men come and go,
like the waves of the sea.
A tear, a prayer to the Great Spirit,
a dirge,
and they are gone from our longing eyes forever.
Even the white man,
whose God walked
and talked with him
as friend to friend,
cannot be exempt from the common destiny.

We may be brothers after all. We shall see.

We will consider your offer. When we have decided, we will let you know.
Should we accept, I here and now make this condition:
we will never be denied the right to visit,
at any time,
the graves of our fathers and friends.

Every part of this earth is sacred to my people.
Every hillside,
every valley,
every clearing and wood,
is holy in the memory and experience of my people.
Even those unspeaking stones along the shore
are loud with the events and
memories in the life of my people.
The ground beneath your feet responds
more lovingly to our steps than yours,
because it is the ashes of our grandfathers.
Our bare feet know the kindred touch.
The earth is rich with the lives of our kin.

The young men, the mothers, and girls,
the little children who once lived and were happy here,
still love these lonely places.
And at evening the forests are dark with the presence of the dead.
When the last red man has vanished from this earth,
and his memory is only a story among the whites,
these shores will still swarm with the invisible dead of my people.
And when your children's children think they are alone
in the fields, the forests,
the shops, the highways,
or the quiet of the woods,
they will not be alone.
There is no place in this country where a man can be alone.
At night when the streets of your towns and cities are quiet,
and you think they are empty,
they will throng with the returning spirits that once thronged them,
and still love those places.
The white man will never be alone.

So let him be just and deal kindly with my people. The dead have power too.

BIBLIOBIGRAPHY

Primary Sources

Arrowsmith, William. 1969. *Speech of Chief Seattle, January 9th, 1855.* Arion 8:461-464.
Arrowsmith, William. 1975. *Speech of Chief Seattle.* The American Poetry Review. p. 23-26.
Perry, Ted. 1991. Letter to Eli Gifford 25, October.
Perry, Ted. 1970. *Home.* Movie script for television series produced by Southern Baptist's
       Radio and Television Commission.
Point Elliott Treaty. National Archives, Washington D.C.
Smith, Henry. 1887. *Scraps from a Diary - Chief Seattle - A Gentleman by Instinct
       - His Native Eloquence.* The Seattle Sunday Star, October 29. p. 10.
The Decidedly Unforked Message of Chief Seattle. 1974. Passages. April.

Secondary Sources

Gifford, Eli. 1992. *The Many Speeches of Chief Seathl: The Manipulation of the Record for Religious, Political, and Environmental Causes.* Occasional papers of Native American Studies I. Sonoma State Uni
  versity, Rohnert Park, California.*
Grant, Frederic James. 18??. Reprinted 1981. *History of Seattle.* New York: American Publishing Co.
Kaiser, Rudolf. 1987. Chief Seattle's Speech(es): American Origins and
  European Reception, In Brian Swann and Arnold Krupat, eds.,
  Recovering the Word, Univ. Calif. Press., Berkeley. pp. 497-536.
Krenmayr, Janice . 1975. *'The earth is our mother' Who really said that?,*
  The Seattle Times Sunday Magazine, January 5. pp. 4-6
Vanderwerth, W. C. 1971. *Indian Oratory.* Norman: University of Okalahoma Press.

*This reference contains a more in-depth study of the history surrounding the speech in its various versions than the background on pages 25-29 of this book. The reference also contains several additional versions of the speech not included in this book.

These fine Native American books are available from your local bookstore or from:

BOOK PUBLISHING COMPANY
PO BOX 99
Summertown TN 38483

Please include $2.50 per book additional for shipping.

If you are interested in other fine books on Native Americans, ecology, alternative health, gardening, vegetarian cooking and childrens' books, please call for a free catalog:

1-800-695-2241